RECHARGE

Your Sales Career With Goal Setting and Time Management

Celia

Hope you make many sales!

Good luck

Carl

by Carl Henry

Cover Design by Alex LaFasto
Book design by Nichole Ward, Morrison Alley Design

Although the author and publisher have made every effort to ensure the accuracy and completeness of information contained in this book, we assume no responsibility for errors, inaccuracies, omissions, or any inconsistency herein. Any slights of people, places, or organizations are unintentional.

First Printing 2009

ISBN 978-0-9817915-3-1

For Will and Virginia

Contents

INTRODUCTION

I really wanted to start this book with the words "goal setting and time management are more important to your sales career than you will probably ever realize." The problem, though, is that you've heard all of that before.

Let's face it, you probably already know that time management and goal setting are important; your sales manager has no doubt mentioned it dozens of times already. So, just as you expect your dentist to tell you to brush more, or for your doctor to recommend more exercise, you think you're ready for what's coming next, and you're all set to nod your head a few times and then move on to something more interesting.

With that in mind, I'll make you a promise – one built on more than twenty five years of sales experience; that if you can take the time to read through this book and make the information a part of your mindset, the advice you'll find will make a *dramatic* difference to what you'll earn over the next five, ten, or fifty years.

How can I make that guarantee? Because I've had the opportunity to work with thousands of salespeople just like you. I've seen what works, and I've seen what fails, too. And from that, I can tell you that where you set your sights, and how you spend the parts of your day, separate the superstars from the average salespeople who just admire them.

So with that, let's get down to business. I wouldn't want to waste anymore time telling you why this is so important to your future when it would just be easier to show you...

> **Time management** *and goal setting aren't about* tips and advice. *They're about creating a plan for where* *you to want to go in life.*

CHAPTER ONE

Taking Control of Your Career

Bruce Lee once famously remarked that anyone could learn kung fu in just five minutes – five minutes here and five minutes there, whenever you get a chance to practice. While I'm not about to test that theory by punching through bricks anytime soon, I bring it up because it speaks directly to the number one challenge facing most salespeople, regardless of their industry, experience, or income level: *how does someone improve their performance and career at a time when we all seem busier than ever?*

The answers to that question, which will fill the remaining pages of this short book, are more than just a bit of helpful advice; they're the keys to a successful sales career. That's because what they amount to isn't just a set of tips, but a comprehensive plan for getting to wherever it is you want to go in your life. Just as a skinny kid with some hours to spare was able to transform himself into a martial arts icon through a consistent, applied effort, you too can start making use of your time and focus to build yourself into something extraordinary.

I want you to pay special attention to those two words: time and focus. You've probably been hearing them your entire life, as most of us have, and yet you may have never given them any real thought. In fact, I'd say that these two concepts, the most powerful tools in your sales arsenal, might be the two that are most overlooked – even amongst established sales professionals.

I see it firsthand all the time. In seminars around the world, I get to meet scores of salespeople every year. The men and women I work with come from different backgrounds, and all have different things that they want to accomplish. But the one thing that they all have, the one common thread, is a dream. Individually, their dreams might be diverse; one person wants to buy a big house by the ocean, while another is saving for a trip around the world. But taken together, it's clear that they're all hoping to turn their sales commissions into something bigger for themselves and their families.

Of course, a handful of these people will turn their dreams into a reality. For most others, though, their dreams will remain just that – fantasies that will never be fulfilled. Much of what I do is aimed at helping these people reach their dreams – and improve their company's bottom line at the same time – by strengthening or enhancing their sales skills. But over the years, I've noticed something interesting: I can only help those who are self-motivated and disciplined. That is, I can give the tools to those who want them, but I can't create that desire to thrive and succeed in another person.

With that in mind, one of the key challenges facing many salespeople out there isn't a lack of ability – it's a lack of motivation. Too many of us are willing to let our dreams sit idle in a corner, waiting for a 'someday' that will never come. I believe that there are some powerful reasons for this. First, most salespeople (and people in general) fail to make a connection between dreams and goals. In other words, they have things that they really want to do in their lives, and things that they know they need to accomplish this week, but there isn't a strong connection between the two. And secondly, I feel that most people never take the time to think about what it is that they *really* want; they have plenty of goals, but none that pull them out of bed in the morning.

We'll address that second issue in just a moment, but for now, I just want to instill the idea that, without goals, we have no direction. We're on the highway, but we're not getting anywhere. This lack of direction is dangerous for any person, but for a salesperson, it can be a career-killer. No amount of sales training can replace desire. Someone who isn't motivated by a personal vision or passion isn't going to be able to find the strength or patience to survive in the world of commission sales; the yellow brick road isn't so fantastic if there's no prize at the end.

In the coming pages, I'm going to do whatever I can to help you find your goals and define them in a way that works for you. Once you've done that, however, you're only halfway there. The second part of this process is learning to manage your time. Most of us waste hours and hours every day doing repetitive and nonessential tasks – time that could be well spent working towards our goals.

Contrary to popular wisdom, time is *not* money. That's because money can be saved for the future, whereas time is spent constantly, second by second, whether you want it to be or not. In that way, it's more like fire or electricity, a powerful force that can be harnessed and utilized, but one that quickly disappears.

Keep that in mind as you flip through these chapters. Everything you get out of life, good or bad, is going to be a reflection of what you put into it. Setting goals and deciding what you want for the future is the first step to actually getting anything done. From there, it's just a matter of finding the most efficient way to it. Using goal-setting and time management isn't just about taking control of your career; it's the way you design and build your future.

The Power of Focus and Consistency

Few salespeople truly appreciate the difference making a consistent effort can make in their lives and careers. The biggest reason for this, I think, is that we get too wrapped up in day-to-day details to see the big picture. There are things we know we should do, but their impact seems so far off that it's hard to find the motivation.

For instance, every salesperson knows that finding new customers – whether it's through referrals, prospecting over the phone, attending networking events, or some other method – is one of the most important things they can do to ensure their long-term success. It's also one of the easiest to skip over when they're busy with meetings, customer service, or one of the thousand other distractions that can come at them throughout their day.

Besides, every producer knows that no single individual call or meeting is likely to transform their career. They're right, of course, in the short term; putting off that call probably isn't going to cost them their job. But seen from the long term, we gain a perspective. Five new contacts a day translates into twenty five new prospects every week. Assuming that you worked 50 weeks a year, that turns into 1,250 possible buyers every twelve months – not to mention their friends, family, colleagues, and other referrals. I don't know of anyone, selling anything in any industry, that wouldn't make a massive improvement in their paycheck with those kinds of numbers. What's more, they could probably find and contact those folks with just half an hour a day.

Of course, we've all heard this before. But what ends up happening is that one thing distracts you, and then another. Sooner or later, those prospects become tomorrow's problem. The net result is a salesperson that is not making nearly as much money as they could be – all because they lack consistency and focus.

This doesn't just work at the office, either. Most of our personal goals can be reached through small, but consistent efforts as well. It's shown again and again that the most effective weight-loss programs, for instance, are those where the participants make gradual changes to their diet and exercise routines. Walking a mile a day – a 15 or 20 minute activity for most people – works out to more than 300 miles per year. Substituting an apple for that mega-sized, extra cream and sugar coffee shake every morning saves tens of thousands of calories over the course of a few months.

I could go on and on with these examples, but hopefully you see what I'm getting at. Becoming truly successful – achieving all of your dreams – doesn't have to take an impossible effort. You just have to be willing to make a few small changes and stick to them. Five minutes – five here, five there, wherever you can find them – of focused effort is better than a lifetime of half-hearted attempts. You can have everything you want in this world, as long as you're willing to keep at it.

> ## *A salesperson is only*
> ### *as good as their motivation,*
> ### *so find the dream that will drive you*
> ## *to sell like a superstar.*

CHAPTER TWO

Give Meaning To Your Goals

Having traveled to most of the larger metropolitan areas in North America, I'm still amazed at the wide variety and types of restaurants that there are out there catering to every taste or craving. I'm not talking about regional specialties, like cheese steaks in Philadelphia or the chili down in Texas. Neither do I mean the exotic fare I sometimes run into, the Szechuan noodle houses found on urban side streets, or the odd falafel hut that thrives a few blocks away from a college campus. No, what I am referring to is the downright weird – and it's out there. I guarantee that no matter what part of the country you live in, there's some eatery within an hour's driving distance that's offering up something unusual. Whether it's seaweed, Rocky Mountain oysters, or even chocolate-covered insects, you can bet that a small crowd of diners is lining up to try.

What's most interesting to me about this isn't the food itself, however; it's the breaking with convention. The simple fact that a handful of people are willing to decide that they'd rather spend their money on something that's been curdled or discarded, rather than enjoying a nice steak or hearty plate of pasta, is fascinating in its own right. In a world where people could choose to eat almost anything, some will go to the extreme to find something that suits their tastes. What's more, they're often willing to drive farther and pay more in the process.

Believe it or not, there's a powerful lesson for salespeople in this: we are all attracted to – and motivated by – different things. What works really well for one person doesn't for another. By virtue of genetics, background, or just plain old personal preference, we all have things that we want. And it's likely that whatever you want isn't exactly the same as what the person next to you wants, or the person next to them for that matter.

So why get into all of this now? Because, as I've already mentioned, a salesperson can only be as good as their motivation. But we're all motivated by different things, and a goal is only worthwhile if it means something to you. I can illustrate what I mean very easily. Ask most people what they're working toward, and the majority of them will tell you that their goal – if they have one at all – is something vague, like 'to have a lot of money.' This is a pretty normal answer. More often than not, it's also complete fluff.

The truth is, most of these people don't even know what they'd do with their imaginary piles of cash. They say it's their goal because it sounds safe and typical, not because they've given it any thought. If you think I'm wrong here, and that most people *do* consider their goals carefully, then I only have to point to real-world examples. Several hundred times a year, men and women around the country win state lotteries that bring them instant riches. What do most of these folks do with their money? Do they live out their dreams happily ever after? Sadly, no. The majority of them spend their winnings and end up back where they started. In fact, quite a few of them overspend, leading to a life that's worse than it was before they got so lucky.

I'm not trying to pick on these people, but rather to make a point: most people don't take the time to really think about what they want. And as a result, they end up with the dreams and goals that they think they *should* have, not the ones that would actually propel them to work harder. As a salesperson, you cannot make this mistake. If you're going to survive the daily routine of prospecting, qualifying, negotiating and closing, then you're going to have to be motivated from within. So take care when choosing which goals and dreams to nurture, and don't feel the pressure to act like you want what everybody else wants. If you're not sure, listen to that voice inside your head. If you're just going through the motions, you'll know it. Even worse, it will show as you struggle to motivate yourself to work every day.

It also helps if you think big. It's sad to say, but there are a lot of men and women out there whose goal is to simply get through each workday. They want to show up, collect a paycheck, and not get hassled by their boss. That's a tough way to go through life, and one that's nearly impossible if you need to generate commissions for a living. Besides, it's no fun. Who wants to simply survive when, as salespeople, we have the tools and skills to make as much money as we want and live out whichever dreams we choose?

So, the next time your sales manager starts talking about that new car you could buy with your production bonus, or the island vacation that's going to the winner of this quarter's sales contest, think carefully about what those things mean to you. If they are luxuries you really want, then by all means use that motivation to keep selling. But if what you really want is a new boat, or a hiking trip to Peru, or even a journey to outer space, then concentrate on that and work towards getting it. Because even though your dream might not mean anything to anyone else, you're never going to achieve it if it doesn't mean something to you.

The hardest part about reaching your goals isn't actually reaching them – it's in discovering what they are in the first place. The world's highest achievers, in sales or any field, are those who have found their passion and are actively working towards it. Find the thing that will really drive you to succeed and you'll be that much closer to actually having it.

Feed Your Dream

Finding what motivates you is a great first step toward becoming a superstar performer, but to give yourself the best chance of getting what you really want, you'll need to reinforce that goal often. That's because the daily challenge of selling – with all of its setbacks and rejections – can push that dream farther and farther back into your mind, until it seems impossible, unrealistic, or just not worth the effort.

So, to recharge your motivation battery, I recommend you do what lots of top performers do: remind yourself of what you're working for, and do it often. That is, keep something around or in front of you all the time that will keep your dream in the front of your mind.

This doesn't mean you have to do anything complicated. In fact, my favorite technique, putting together a "goal board," shouldn't take you more than half an hour to set up for yourself. Basically, a goal board is a collection of pictures and articles – mostly cut out from magazines and the Internet – that represent things you'd like to have or experience. For some salespeople, this could be a house or a boat; for others, it could be pictures of the place where they'd like to have their dream vacation or retirement.

If you've never put a goal board together before, you might be surprised at how fun and motivating it can be. The first step is to do things I advised in this chapter – think about what it is you'd really like to have, which dreams you're truly driven to fulfill. Next, take a trip down to your local bookstore or newsstand. Find magazines aimed at that interest, and especially those with lots of big pictures you can use. Web pages can work, too, but you'll want to find a way of printing the images you see. That's because, once you've amassed a dozen or so photos that remind you of your dream, you're going to cut them out and glue them onto a large piece of poster paper. The exact size doesn't matter, so long as it fits somewhere on a wall very near your desk.

Finally, when you've finished arranging your goal board, you're ready for the easiest – and most powerful – part of the process. Simply place your goal board up somewhere in your field of vision. This should be a place where you can't help but see it first thing in the morning, when you're on the phone, or preparing for a client meeting. That's because those images that you chose are going to serve as a constant reminder of what you're working for.

It's a simple trick, but one that works extraordinarily well. Any time you deal with a tough prospect, or narrowly miss out on closing a sale, all you have to do is look up at that board and let it give you the energy to keep pushing ahead.

Having a visual reminder of your goals is one of the easiest and best ways to keep yourself pushing forward. So, take my advice and break out the scissors and glue. Arranging a goal board isn't just a great way to focus on your dreams – it can help you find the energy to reach them, too.

The first step *toward becoming a top salesperson is* *to start believing* *that you're ready to become one.*

CHAPTER THREE

Creating Confidence

I'm something of an optimist by nature. Lots of prominent psychologists would argue that this is an inborn trait, that some people will naturally see the glass as half full. In my case, however, I think that my outlook on life comes from history and experience. While the world certainly seems to have it share of problems, I'm always comforted by the knowledge that humans have overcome monumental challenges in the past.

Take, for instance, the case of heavier than air flight. At the turn of the last century, this issue was a very big deal. Much like cold fusion energy or advanced cancer treatments, it was the cutting edge technology of its day – not quite achieved, but seemingly within our grasp.

Nowadays, of course, flying is a pretty old trick. Anyone not living in a secluded jungle somewhere knows that it works, and modern aircraft can allow you to start your day on one end of the world and finish it on the other. In fact, unless it's your first trip, there is very little that's even all that exciting about the experience anymore. But it's good to remember that things weren't always this way – that people didn't used to fly, and that a large percentage of the population even considered it to be *impossible*.

The skeptics weren't just confined to laypeople, either. Some of the best minds of the time – great engineers, professors, and physicists – flatly stated that it couldn't be done; no object heavier than air could overcome the force of gravity. And really, their analysis made sense. If you threw a stone in the sky, it was pretty certain to come down. So the thought of a thousand ton jumbo jet hurtling above the clouds near the speed of sound would have seemed downright ridiculous.

So what made the difference for the Wright brothers and their successors in aviation? The simple truth is that they looked beyond their own experience and into what they were sure could be done. In other words, they saw birds flying and thought "Well, if they can do it, so can we!" From there, it took some serious work and innovation to get their flyer off the ground, but it all started with the attitude that they could and would succeed.

I'm mentioning all of this because without confidence in your own ability to reach your dreams, you'll never find the kind of success you should be looking for. If you don't have the internal belief that you can accomplish what you set out to do, it will remain an impossibility, no matter how hard you try. In other words, if, in your heart of hearts, you don't feel like you're good enough, smart enough, or driven enough to get what you want, you never will.

This is an easy issue to understand, but a harder one to master. That's because most of us have a natural comfort level when it comes to success, a baseline that we tend to gravitate towards. And, more often than not, it's dictated by whatever we're used to.

For instance, if you've spent your entire adult life working for minimum wage at a gas station, you might have a very difficult time envisioning yourself as a multimillionaire with a large estate. If, on the other hand, you were raised in the lap of luxury, it's probably going to be a lot easier to become comfortable with plush surroundings.

Now, I'm not making the case that the person at the bottom of the economic food chain can't climb to the top. Indeed, the thing that I love most about our country – and especially the sales profession – is that anyone can decide where they're going to end up. What I am saying is that we all carry ideas of who we are, and what we're going to do, and that these ideas can propel us forward or hold us back; if you're going to be a top performer, you'll need to think of yourself as one.

Luckily, there are a number of things you can do to make that happen. The first, and easiest, is to spend your time with other sales superstars. Top salespeople are great motivators. Not only are they filled with knowledge about their profession, but they have an excitement about their work that tends to be contagious. More than that, they just seem to emanate their belief that anything is possible. Hang around with them enough, and their attitudes will probably start to rub off on you.

Another good idea is to take 10 or 15 minutes each morning and read or listen to something positive and motivational. Sometimes, just thinking about what other people have accomplished in their careers is enough to get your day off on the right foot. And, as we saw in the last chapter, that's all it really takes to be successful – finding something that works and doing a little bit of it every day.

One final technique that I've always liked, and one that works for lots of people, is to simply take a few moments here and there to visualize yourself as a success. This concept is so simple that many people choose to disregard it entirely, even though it's a favorite of many of the world's greatest achievers, regardless of their field. In fact, visualization works so well that it's not uncommon for sports teams and national Olympic programs to bring in facilitators who help athletes to imagine themselves giving the performance of a lifetime. It's also been utilized by military units and Fortune 500 companies to break through barriers. The simple reason? It works.

If you want to give it a try, all you have to do is sit back in a comfortable spot and close your eyes. Take a few deep breaths, and once you relax, mentally run through your day. Simply think of all the challenges you're likely to face, and then see yourself overcoming them. Imagine what it will feel like having just successfully reached a handful of important prospects, or negotiated a particularly large sale. The process doesn't have to take a long time or be very complicated in order to work. All you're trying to do is to let your brain become comfortable with the idea of doing well. Once you get back to work, things will be that much easier because you've already imagined a great day – now all you have to do is reproduce it.

Creating confidence in yourself and your own long-term success isn't that difficult to do, but it is important. Without that sense that you're bound to succeed – the inner belief that you are a superstar salesperson – you're going to have a hard time getting anywhere in your career.

Find a Mentor

I've already stated my belief that one of the easiest ways to create confidence is to hang out with other successful people. Seeing what they've done and accomplished is a surefire way to prove to yourself that you can reach your own dreams. But if you want to take that one step further, and make your career a lot easier in the process, then I suggest you go and find a good mentor.

I've already covered many of the reasons you should find a more experienced salesperson to guide you and offer advice in my other books, and they all still stand. A good mentor can help you grow and develop in your career at a much faster rate than you'd be able to do on your own. They've been where you are, they can point out the shortcuts to take and pitfalls to avoid. And even when they can't help you solve a problem out right, they can lend an ear and remind you that you'll live to fight again.

More than that, though, a good mentor – especially one who is similar to you in a few ways – can serve as a living reminder of what can be done. There's nothing so motivating as seeing another man or woman, who might have started out with the same talents and personality traits as you, make it to the top of the pile. Even without all of their advice and guidance, their success makes the time you spend with them worthwhile. Every new sale, every bonus, and every commission check they earn can help you keep your chin up and your confidence high.

Of course, for this to work you're going to have to choose a mentor who is successful. It's a good idea to find someone who has a positive attitude, and one who is willing to invest a little time in you and your career. This is usually easier than you might think. Most men and women who make it to the top of any profession, and especially sales, have gotten to where they are because they have a positive outlook and aren't shy about taking on the challenges ahead of them. Show them that you would like to learn to do the same, and you'll probably find a new friend and an invaluable resource.

Goals are where the

rubber meets the road.

They're your bridge

to the future.

CHAPTER FOUR

Setting Motivational Goals

So far, I've asked you to spend a lot of time looking forward. There's a good reason for this. Most people never think about what they're truly motivated to achieve, and because of that, they never know how close they could be to getting it. And besides, as you'll see again in this chapter, dreams and goals are only as useful as they are motivating. It's only by peeking into the future that we can find the strength to accomplish more today. Still, to get into the proper frame of mind to look at goal setting, we're going to have to switch gears. Instead of peering farther and farther forward, we're going to do the reverse and work backward.

In my experience, goals are misunderstood things. They aren't your dreams or wants, the ultimate rewards for your hard work. No, goals are where the rubber meets the road; they are the map of the terrain, the way to use your work to get to the things you really want. They're a bridge between the present and the future. For that reason, I like to take a bit of a different approach to goals. Rather than think about what it is you want to do, or are expected by your sales manager to do, I'd encourage you to work backwards. That is, start with those dreams you thought so much about, and are working so hard to nurture. Whether it's a quiet place in the country, a portfolio stuffed with blue chip investments, or that luxury car, picture the thing you've set your heart on having. Like I said, finding that spark is the hard part; the rest is simple math.

What will it take for you to reach your dream? More specifically, how much money will you need to earn, and how soon? These figures, transformed into meaningful targets, are a big part of the process, so if you don't know, find out. Search online, talk to a salesperson, visit a dealer – do whatever you have to do to find out what you're really going to need. Once you have, write that number at the top of a piece of paper. This is going to be the dollar amount that you need to raise in order to reach your dream. Whether it's ten dollars, ten thousand, or ten million isn't the point; knowing what you're aiming for is.

It's important to point out that right now isn't the time to be reasonable. If your ultimate dream is to buy a private island that costs fifteen million dollars, and that's what you really want out of life, then write it down. A good motivational goal is any one that drives you forward, so now is no time to censor your wishes.

Next, attach a timeline to your goal. Decide how long you think it should take you to reach. This is an area where common sense should come into play. If you're deeply in debt, then buying a Ferrari next week is probably going to be next to impossible. On the other hand, never set your dreams so far out that it feels like you're never going to reach them. A dream that's too far into the future isn't all that motivating; you need something that's going to compel you to work today.

This is where the working backwards part comes into play. Take that dream, and the price tag you attached to it, and divide by the number of years or months you want to reach it in. As an example, your dream might be a beach house that costs half a million dollars, and you'd like to buy it within ten years. You now know that you need to save fifty thousand dollars per year. This becomes your intermediate goal.

How many new accounts will you have to open in order to meet that figure? If you know, write it down. If you don't, find someone who does, or make your best estimate. Every industry and territory are a bit different, but the chances are good that you or your sales manager has calculated the average value of each of your accounts (which is helpful information for you to know anyway), so you can use that to get pretty close to an exact figure.

From there, you just have to figure out how many calls, letters, appointments, or other activities you're going to have to generate to find those new clients. For instance, let's say that you sell industrial equipment and supplies, and that your average new client nets you $2,500 in commissions. Certainly, you'll have bigger orders and smaller ones, but you've calculated that most of them will come in somewhere around that number. From that basis, you can infer that you'll need to find twenty new customers – about one every two and a half weeks – if you're going to meet your goals. If you know that you need to call on five prospects to get one appointment, and that for each five you meet, you'll typically close one into new business, then you can say with confidence that you're going to have to make five hundred calls (since it takes twenty-five to find a new client) in order to reach your goal.

Could you make ten calls a week to achieve your greatest dream? Would you make twenty, or even fifty? If you wouldn't, then one of two things is probably going on. In the first case, you might just not be cut out for sales. This is a field where the truly self-driven succeed, and if the idea of having what you want most in life won't compel you to find new business, then there probably isn't anything that will.

That being said, it's more likely you just haven't found whatever it is that you really want yet. For whatever reason, either because you haven't thought about it long enough, or you're afraid to admit to yourself what you really desire, you've just failed to hit on your true motivator. Once people find their passion in life, and the way to get to it, they tend to be relentless in their pursuit. So, if your dream doesn't give you the urge to sell, it's probably just not the right one for you. Remember, your goals are just going to be daily, weekly, and quarterly targets that carry you to your dream – make sure they're leading you somewhere you actually want to go.

What's Realistic?

Talk about goals for very long, or read one of the hundreds of books on setting goals, and you'll soon run into an interesting question: how important is it that goals be *realistic*? What's more important, keeping your eyes on the stars, or your feet on the ground?

The best answer is both. No one should ever be dissuaded from following what they feel is their passion or calling. If you need to sell twenty million units of your product, which is more than anyone's ever done before, to get what you want, then I say by all means do it! Don't let other peoples' ideas of what can be done – or even your own – get in the way of reaching your dream.

On the other hand, you don't want to drive yourself crazy over a goal that you aren't going to be able to reach. How do you tell the difference? In my mind, it's all about your timeline. I personally believe that any person who commits themselves to becoming a superstar salesperson is capable of earning incredible amounts of money. I also, however, believe that few people become sales legends, or quadruple their income, overnight.

So the answer is to reach for the most audacious thing you can think of, if it's what you want, but to make your intermediate goals a little closer to home. If your dream is to make a million dollars a year, but you're only making a twentieth of that now, then why not make it your quarterly goal to increase your income by 25%? That increase should be enough to push you, but not so great that it feels like something you can't achieve. Just as it's dangerous to have no goal, you shouldn't have one that you don't think you can ever reach, either. To set goals that way just encourages you to disregard them and fail. Once you do that, the next goal seems less real, and then the next, and so on and on.

Likewise, if you find that you have a dream that can most likely only be reached with decades of hard work, then make a compromise with yourself. Keep your dream intact – never discard the thing that really drives you on – but find a couple of more immediate dreams, as well. For instance, if you're fantasizing about a yacht that you know will take many, many years of hard work to buy, then why not set a shorter-term goal to rent one for a long weekend? That way, you can keep working towards your dream, while giving yourself something more immediate to work for, not to mention a reward for your hard work, in the meantime.

Set yourself up to succeed by choosing short-term goals that are achievable, and long-term goals that satisfy your inner hunger. Few people are going to realistically make hundreds of cold calls in a week, so don't write that down as your short term goal if it's just going to discourage you. In the same way, don't be afraid to plan to achieve the things you really want. Even the greatest triumphs are accomplished through small, consistent efforts; the prize is always there if you're willing to keep after it.

"*Time wasted is*
gone forever."

CHAPTER FIVE

Managing Your Time

In my neck of the woods, colonial history is a big deal. In fact, you can hardly stroll too far through any town or village along the eastern sea board without being reminded of our country's heritage by some statue, plaque, or monument. Some of them point out places of interest, like early settlements, or the beginnings of our democracy. Others commemorate famous explorers who crossed the oceans in ships that seemed too small and rickety to survive a stiff breeze, much less a trek across the sea to a new continent.

Because of the history involved, I used to take my son to some of these places when he was younger. Not only was it a good teaching environment, but I think most kids are rightly impressed with stories about battles and conquistadors. For me, though, the real story has always been behind the scenes. As fantastic as the historical accomplishments were, all the stuff that happened before they ever left the shore is just as amazing.

That's because, for every one of those great voyages began by some great explorer, a lot of seemingly minor decisions had to be made – decisions that meant the difference between life and death. Looking ahead to a journey that might span weeks over the ocean, and then years in the wilderness, these explorers had to learn to appropriate space in a way that seems unimaginable now. Do you bring more gunpowder, or save the room for fresh water? What will be more useful in the new world, a few silver coins or an extra pair of boots? I'd have to imagine that it's pretty difficult to anticipate everything you're going to need when you only have a space the size of a closet, especially when there are no 24 hour supermarkets or convenience stores along your scheduled route. Given the long-term implications of those tradeoffs, I used to often wonder whether it was those decisions about small wooden barrels that kept the explorers up at night, as much as any fear of sea monsters or angry natives.

In a way, though, I also have to think that those decisions were that much easier, if only because the captains grasped the importance of each one. Let me explain: those explorers knew they had to ration their space carefully. To be careless meant to disappear and become a footnote in history. Therefore, everything was given the proper amount of thought and planning.

Contrast that with the way most salespeople spend the one thing they can reliably turn into money and a stronger future: *their time.* Rather than think carefully about what they'll need, and how it can carry them ahead, they toss it into the wind and hope it will drift back. Walk into any of the thousands of sales offices or bullpens around the world, and you'll see exactly what I mean. While a few men and women will be working hard, focused on their daily goals, the majority will lose hours a day to the Internet, e-mail, long phone calls, and pointless meetings.

In the first chapter, I tried to impress upon you that even the most minor changes in your daily routine, things as simple as making a few calls or finding a moment to improve upon your sales skills, can lead to dramatic results over the long term. But this principle works both ways. A few bad habits – like spending too much time reading the paper or surfing through web sites – can add up to thousands of lost hours every year. That's time you could be using to reach, or even exceed, your daily goals.

For that reason, it's absolutely critical that you get a grip on where your time is going. Every one of us only gets so many productive hours every day, week, and year. What you choose to do with them dictates everything about your sales career. How much money will you make? What kind of future will you build for your family? How satisfied would you be with what you've accomplished? You're answering those questions every time you choose to do, or not do, the activities that will generate meetings and appointments for you and your company.

In the next chapter, we're going to look at a few basic ways that you can recoup some of the precious hours and days you're missing. In some cases, they'll probably be things you know you should be taking care of, but could use the reminder. Other times, you might not even be aware of how much time you are wasting. For now, though, I just want to make sure you understand the main point – that time wasted is gone forever. No single tip or idea is as important as grasping that concept. Once you really get that finding an extra half hour a day can be worth hundreds of thousands of dollars over the course of your sales career, finding those minutes becomes a lot easier.

Believe it or not, you're on a journey in your sales career. And, like the explorers of old, you aren't going to get many chances to get it right; your window of opportunity to make it to the next shore is slimmer than you think. Every morning when you wake up, you're filling those wooden barrels with minutes. Whether you put enough in them to sustain you and help you reach your destination is up to you, but I hope you'll think long and hard about what to bring.

Getting the Most Out of Your Days

The real key to effective time management is focus. Doing the right things, and getting them done in a timely way, can give you a massive edge over your peers and competitors, and so I advise you to use *all* your time carefully, not just your office hours.

Think about the sales superstars you know. I'm willing to bet these men and women are some of the first in the office, and among the last to leave. But, I'd also be willing to wager that they don't live in their offices. That is, despite their laser focus, these folks usually have a number of interests that lie outside of their work life. They might be involved in various charities, or have hobbies and interests that they have devoted their evenings and weekends to. In short, they found a few things outside of sales that make them happy.

If you're going to be truly successful, and not burn out a few years into your sales career, then you're going to need to take their example to heart. It's easy, with all the thought about goals and achievement, to think that everything should come down to finding new clients and business. But the truth is that the best salespeople aren't just top producers – they're happy, well-rounded individuals.

Someone who is excited about their life brings a positive energy and attitude to everything they do, and clients can pick up on this. Likewise, somebody who's wound so tightly that they can only focus on their next commission, even when they should be enjoying a weekend or vacation, will tend to repel customers. So, as contradictory as it might sound, sometimes the best thing you can do to help your sales is to do anything but sell.

Where should you draw the line? Chances are that you'll know when you get there. Time spent exercising, eating right, or having a break now and then is never wasted. If, on the other hand, you're just looking for an excuse to slack off, you'll feel it inside. When it comes to deciding when to make room for yourself, just follow your gut. More often than not, it knows what you need, and so will you.

*"**Saving a few minutes** each morning can net you extra days and weeks every year."*

CHAPTER SIX

Eleven Time Management Tips

It's kind of a bit ironic that some of the best material available on time management can take hours to learn and apply. With that in mind, I'd like to offer you a handful of guidelines that have served me well over the years. While I'm certainly not an expert in the field, and would recommend you try some other books and CDs on the subject, these tips should help you find more time in your workday for the important things:

Use a calendar or schedule.

Approaching your day without any kind of plan is a bit like cold calling randomly from the phone book – you might accomplish something, but it's going to be about a hundred times harder than it should be. You don't need to use an expensive program or planner to get yourself organized. Just be sure you start each day, week, and month with a good idea of what you need to get done, and then map out a way to finish it in your available hours.

Start with your goals.

If you've followed my advice up to this point, then your goals aren't just some arbitrary target that you want to hit – they're the blueprint to achieving your dream. So, when you start to build your calendar for the day or week, be sure you leave enough time to do the things you promised yourself you'd finish. Remember, your goal isn't something you achieve all at once; it's the result of dozens, hundreds, or even thousands of days' worth of consistent effort.

Do important things first.

If there's something that you know you absolutely have to get done, either because it's important or urgent, then do it first. Having it finished will take a huge psychological burden off your shoulders, and you're less likely to rush through the most critical project of the day.

Concentration is critical.

There came a time, right around the invention of handheld PDAs, where most of the business world picked up the notion that successful people are always busy. Not only were they busy, in fact, but they were doing lots of different things at once. If you couldn't have lunch with a client while simultaneously e-mailing your sales manager and getting text messages from your spouse, you probably weren't doing enough – or so the theory went. What one study after another has found since, however, is that humans have one-track minds. We do our best stuff when we're concentrating on what's right in front of us. I'm not telling you to completely shut yourself off from multitasking, which is pretty impractical advice for most of us, but to focus as much as possible. You'll actually do a lot more, in much shorter time, than you would if you tried to tackle everything at once.

Know when you're good.

Every one of use has an internal clock that differs. Some of us are morning people, and do our best work when the sun is coming up. Others of us are night owls, and like burning the midnight oil. You should try, within reason, to do your most creative and energetic tasks (like giving in-person presentations or making sales calls) during those times when you feel most energetic. Save other jobs, like paperwork, for the parts of the day when you aren't as sharp.

Don't work for minimum wage.

Readers of my book *15 Hot Tips That Will Supercharge Your Sales Career* will recognize this one immediately, but it's an important point. As a professional salesperson, you get paid to generate new business, and this activity is, by far, the most profitable thing you can do. So why do so many salespeople waste so many hours cleaning, typing, filing, and doing other minimum wage jobs? There are literally dozens of places to hire help for those tasks, and at very reasonable rates, so put your time and energy into finding new business. The extra income it brings you will offset the expense dozens of times over.

Be productive, not busy.

The best part of sales is that no one but you can decide what you're going to earn this year. The worst part of sales is that it's usually completely up to you to make it happen. Even the best sales manager in the world can't keep that close an eye on their team, so if you decide to give less than your full effort, there's probably no one to stop you. I think that's why so many salespeople waste hours and days organizing their desks or fine-tuning sales presentations beyond what they need – those actions make them look and feel busy, even if they're not getting much done. You're only going to get so many hours, days, and weeks in a year; use them to reach your goals, not doing busywork.

Get repetitive.

In your company and industry, there are probably dozens of requests, questions, or issues that come up again and again. Rather than eat up your productive hours dealing with the same thing over and over, why not create a single file or response that tackles it? As an example, if you find that customers e-mail you frequently to ask about the pricing of a particular model or add-on, and you always give the same answer, then why not create one e-mail for that purpose? Any time that request comes in, you can simply take a moment to personalize it and hit 'send,' rather than dealing with each one personally. Of course, there are probably dozens of other ways you could apply this, but the point is to look for repetitive parts of your job and make them automatic, so you can free up your time for other things.

Guard your time.

You may have coworkers or friends who aren't as concerned about their productivity as you are about yours. The key to dealing with them isn't to be cold or dismissive – you should have an active personal life, and even if you don't, maintaining good relationships is always a part of sales. Instead, if a conversation, visit, or lunch is going on a bit too long, simply explain that you have work to do, or an appointment to get to, and offer to meet or follow up later. The idea is to be working when you're working, so you can be free when you aren't.

Weed out your inbox.

A good gardener keeps weeds away by removing them at the first sign. What I recommend is that you treat your inbox the same way. Looking at a huge backlog of messages isn't just discouraging and fatiguing; it makes it hard to find what you're looking for. So, something new comes to your desk – whether it's on a letter, scribbled in a note, or flashing on your screen – either file it, deal with it, or get rid of it right away. And speaking of which...

Set aside time.

You know that you'll have to devote a certain number of minutes or hours each day to dealing with mail, e-mail, and phone calls, so why not schedule for those things? By giving yourself time to follow up on these tasks, you'll be less tempted to bother with them when you should be doing something else. As an added benefit, you'll probably waste less time on each because you're concentrating.

Rules are made to be broken

I've included a handful of time management tips in this chapter, and I sincerely believe they could help any salesperson reach his or her goals more quickly. And if you really take your career seriously, you could check out any one of a number of leading books on the topic and find even more great advice. But while I recommend you learn and practice the basics, I would also point out that it's just as important to know when to *break* the rules as it is to follow them.

Just like prospecting, negotiating, or closing, time management is an inexact skill. What works well for one person won't necessarily fly for another. For one thing, we all have our own personal work habits. While a certain expert might recommend getting up at the crack of dawn to write sales proposals, that could be terrible advice for the producer who isn't much of a morning person and is barely coherent until their third cup of coffee.

Additionally, some tips just don't work as well in the real world as they do on paper. For instance, nearly every time management guru I've ever run across, whether in print or through a seminar, has recommended keeping a time log. For a specified period of time, usually a week or two, you're supposed to write down every activity you perform, along with the time of day and number of minutes it takes you. I have no trouble believing this is a wonderful activity that will yield all kinds of valuable personal and professional insights. There's only one problem – nobody does it. Few people have the memory and persistence to document their every move, and so the advice becomes meaningless.

There are also times when you want to consider the bigger picture. Keeping your e-mail closed, for example, is generally a good idea. With the dozens, or even hundreds, of messages that most busy salespeople receive each day, an open inbox can be a constant distraction that stops you from finishing more important work. That being said, I can think of a recent occasion where breaking that rule probably saved me hours of work and follow up later.

It was a late afternoon, and I had been waiting for a response from a contact of mine who was in senior management. When I saw his e-mail, in which he asked a quick question, pop up on my screen, I realized he must be in the office. By giving him a quick call when I knew he was available, I was able to make personal contact and close the sale. Had I not checked my inbox right away to look for new messages, I might have had to wait another week to find a good time to reach him. And who knows, during that time they might have changed their budget, decided not to hold the meeting, or even been contacted by one of my competitors. I can't say that being prompt made that sale for me, but it certainly didn't hurt.

At the end of the day, time management tips only work as well as you use them. With that in mind, don't be afraid to try new ideas and strategies for getting more out of your day. But just as importantly, keep what works for you and discard the rest. Having time management tips that irritate you, or distract you from selling, is almost as bad as having none at all.

> **Time management** shows you how to free up some of your day. Efficiency teaches you *to use it wisely.*

CHAPTER SEVEN

Becoming Effecient

In the same way that many people mistake dreams for goals, they also tend to confuse time management with efficiency. If dreams are the things you truly want out of life, then goals are the way to get you there. Similarly, if time management is learning how to free up more of your time, then efficiency is about using it wisely. One has everything to do with doing things better, but the other tells you what you should be doing in the first place.

Luckily for me, salespeople tend to increase their efficiency as they become more experienced. This can show itself in a number of ways. For example, whereas a rookie producer, full of enthusiasm, will often make calls to anyone who has a phone to find appointments, the veteran can usually produce the same results in a tenth of the time – simply by calling on prospects who are likely to buy. There isn't any magic in this; it's simply being smarter with your time by leveraging your efforts.

Another trait of savvy sales veterans is that they tend to listen more than they talk. I've covered this pretty exhaustively in my other books, so I won't dwell on it except to say that every prospect in the world will tell you everything you need to know – including what they want to buy, when they want to buy it, or if they're even a good prospect to begin with – if you just give them the chance. Still, a lot of salespeople never grow out of the tendency to talk. They want to talk about features, about their company, and about themselves, when all they'd have to do to make a sale is to listen. Good listening is the very peak of efficiency, because it allows you to maximize your sales while minimizing your effort.

And speaking of quiet, be sure to give yourself some once in a while. That is, take a moment to stop and think about what you're doing, why you're doing it, and how well it's working. I'm always amazed at how few salespeople know the numbers in their own business: how many calls it takes to set an appointment, how many appointments for a sale, the average commission on a new account, and so on. Without that data, how can you decide where to devote your energies? Granted, you should always be moving forward and trying to generate sales, but never get so busy that, you forget about the planning.

It's also a good idea to remember that there are a lot of things you can do – like cultivating relationships, speaking to groups, or becoming an expert in your field – that might not lead to more sales in the short-term, but can bring dramatic improvements over the length of your career. If you've checked out any of my other books or materials, you already know that I'm a big proponent of continuing education. The day you stop learning about sales, about your products and your company, is the day you stop getting any better. And consequently, once you stop getting better, you usually stop increasing your income at the same time. Take a few minutes to pick up a book or a CD; those small tips you pick up along the way can double or triple your production over time.

Just as some of the best things you can do for your sales career don't actually involve selling directly, remember that many of your greatest ideas can come when you're not looking for them. Early in my career, I used to spend a few minutes brainstorming each morning on the one question that I was sure would define me as a salesperson: *what can I do to increase my value to my customers?* Sometimes I would have a great thought, and sometimes I wouldn't. But by going through the exercise, I created an environment where I was always subconsciously thinking about improving my sales. As a result, a lot of creative solutions came to me when I wasn't expecting them, and they often led to me adding new clients that I wouldn't otherwise have had.

By the same token, I think that one of the most efficient things I do is leave the office early once in a while. That might sound a bit contradictory, but if I reach my goal for the day or week, why not give my mind a rest? Having a bit of downtime here and there keeps things fresh for me, and it also allows me to enjoy the benefits of a flexible sales schedule.

I know that some of you are probably thinking that you don't have that kind of latitude in your own office, that your hours are set by someone else. I would answer that you probably have more freedom than you think you do – so long as you follow the rest of the advice in this book and use it to your advantage. If you find the dream in life that will guide you to action, create a yearly, monthly and daily plan to achieve it, and then cut out the time-wasting activities that hold you back, you're going to be several times more productive than your peers. Once you achieve that level of success, do you think your sales manager is going to be worried about where you are on a Friday afternoon? Of course not. There are limits, but top performers get the flexibility they desire because they're self-motivated. Managers know they'll hit their numbers, and so they give them the freedom to perform.

As I've said many times in the past, sales is not a real job. You don't get a check for showing up, or even for trying as hard as you can. Until somebody spends some money on the product or service you're selling, you haven't made anything happen. Whether that takes an hour or a year is irrelevant, because it's not how much time you put in, but the quality. Remember that and don't just sell as much as you can – sell it as efficiently as possible.

Qualifying and Customer Service Equal Time and Money

Perhaps the biggest thing salespeople can do to produce more efficiently – to truly work smarter and not harder – is to become better qualifiers. That's because learning to separate the serious buyers from the imposters, locating customers and turning away "tire kickers," can save you untold hours, effort, and money.

Again, this is an area where those of us who have been around the block once or twice have a leg up. We know from experience how long it takes to cultivate every good lead. There might be dozens of phone calls, multiple meetings, several proposals, and days or weeks' worth of follow up and negotiation just to pull in a single new account – not to mention time and budgets used on things like travel and samples. Why waste all of that on a prospect that could have been ruled out by asking one more question?

And if qualifying is the number one efficiency booster, then customer service has to come in a close second. It's surprising how many folks haven't figured this one out; they grumble when their clients call because they think it's taking them away from their more profitable activities. They're right, of course, *at the moment.* Telling a customer about the features of a product they've already bought isn't likely to generate a new sale that afternoon.

However, by going the extra mile and always being there for the people who buy from them, they make it very difficult for competing salespeople to steal accounts. Again, think of the time, effort, and attention that went into winning that business. Why throw that away by not doing the kind of follow up that could have kept them on the books? Besides, it's very rare that any of us ever sells a product that doesn't eventually need to be replaced or upgraded. Do the right thing today, whether it takes five minutes or five hours, and you'll already be halfway to making the next sale to that same client – not to mention anyone who asks them for a referral.

A wise man once said that the wisdom of life is eliminating the nonessentials, and that's exactly what qualifying and customer service are all about. Spending less time prospecting from scratch, when you could be focused on qualified leads and existing customers, isn't just efficient – it's the way to build a monster career.

> *Never underestimate* the power of a *focused and determined mind.* "

CHAPTER EIGHT

Keeping Your Eyes on the Road

I must admit that, as a professional speaker who spends a lot of time on the road, there are certain technologies that I can't quite remember how we ever lived without. Cell phones and laptop computers, for instance, come to mind right away, as do wireless microphones and Internet capabilities. But what I'm really thinking about right now is something a bit more basic – GPS navigation systems.

For most of my career, traveling to a seminar meant packing up my things, boarding a flight, and then driving the remainder of the way through small towns and state highways, often with handwritten directions from a client or meeting planner. As you might imagine, this system led to as many detours and wasted hours as it did efficient trips. That's because, no matter how good the directions were, you always had to watch out for road construction, unidentified streets, closed exits, and so on.

That's all in the past now. Whenever I arrive in a new city these days, all I have to do is walk to a rental counter, take a shuttle to my car, and then plug in the address I want to end up at. From there, computers and satellites do the rest. Not only do they guide me efficiently to my destination, but they warn me of delays – along with restaurants and attractions – that might change my intended route. In short, I make a plan, but the GPS helps me to stay on it, and in the most efficient way possible.

Could we build a better metaphor for the way we should be approaching our sales careers? Never treat your dreams and goals as a simple "start here and end there" kind of journey. There are simply too many things that can happen along the way – those unexpected victories and setbacks that can jump out while you're driving – to go along on cruise control. In order for your dreams and goals to work for you, you're going to need to keep your eyes on the map, but you can't afford to lose sight of the road while you do it.

You might think, having already said so much about setting your goals, that I wouldn't need to bring this up again, but the fact of the matter is that most of us treat our goals as a sort of starting line. Once the work of achieving them begins, we just put our heads down and keep barreling forward. Ironically, it's the very best salespeople who are the most susceptible. They're so good at motivating themselves that they start to follow a predictable pattern: decide what they want, and then keep pushing themselves until they get it.

Some of our dreams, however, can take years, decades, or lifetimes to reach. For that reason, it's a good idea to take some time here and there to think about your dreams and goals. Do they still excite you? Are you still on track to reach them? Taking a few minutes a month to have that discussion with yourself can go a long way towards not only making you a happier, more fulfilled human being, but a stronger salesperson, as well. Why? Because if you've lost the passion for the dream you're chasing, that's going to come through in the way you approach your work.

At the same time, the shifting nature of human desires is a good reason to have long and short term goals. If you decide you no longer want to save for that beach house in Maui, or were never sure what you wanted in the first place, then having something more immediate to shoot for can help keep you motivated to pull the best out of yourself. Besides, it's hard to be motivated on a daily basis for something you've promised yourself in twenty or thirty years. That's not to say that you should discard those dreams, only that you should have other, more immediate things you want to accomplish along the way. In that way, short-term goals, even though they might not be as powerful as your grander dreams, can be even more motivating and refreshing.

Perhaps the strongest reason to keep reassessing your goals, though, is one you might not have even thought of – that you'll need something new to chase when you achieve your dreams. If there's one mistake people tend to make the most, it's probably to set their goals too low. They're afraid to dream of the things they really want, and so they settle for something that seems more 'realistic.' But by learning to push themselves forward, a little bit at a time, they often reach their goal more quickly than they thought possible.

Don't underestimate yourself, or the power of a focused mind. People have amassed great fortunes, built enormous empires, and achieved works of amazing genius just by being clear about what they were trying to do. I'm willing to bet that, whatever your dreams are, they aren't any more audacious than that. So dream big, and when you achieve it, aim even higher.

Sales, like most of life's pursuits, requires equal parts desire, belief, and effort. I hope that the advice in this book has helped you find a little more of each, and that you'll take that and use it to get everything you ever dreamed of – and then a little more.

For Sales Managers

If you're a sales manager looking through this book for the first time, or better yet, going through it with your team, you're probably seeing a lot of things that you've been trying to instill in your sales force for a long time. And to that end, I hope you've found this material to be a big help in getting them moving in the right direction.

At the same time, I want to point out that there are a few steps you can take to help that process along, especially with the newer producers on your staff. Commission sales isn't easy; it's not unusual for people who haven't done it before to lose their focus or become overwhelmed. As the manager, you're the one who's going to have to bring them back into the fold. Here are a couple of things I've picked up along the way:

Try to reward results over activity. Sales managers tend to love stats, and I can understand why. Looking over the number of cold calls, meetings, or proposals a salesperson has produced can be a great way to see how they're doing – especially when you have a group that's so large it's tough to keep tabs on each producer personally. Keep in mind, though, that activity can be deceiving. I've seen more than one case where an efficient salesperson constantly exceeded their goals only to be criticized by their manager for not making enough calls. Likewise, you will probably have men or women on your staff who fill their days calling on or meeting with prospects who will never buy, simply because they're poor qualifiers.

Your department exists to sell – which method your team takes isn't nearly as important as the result.

Secondly, do what you can to help your team set goals that suit the level they're at in their careers. A goal that is too easy to reach is meaningless, because it doesn't require them to stretch at all. On the other end of the spectrum, setting goals that are impossible to get leads to a cycle of failures, and the end result is always an unproductive team that resents you for placing unrealistic demands on them. Each member of your team should always be pushing and growing to be better, and little improvements, compounded over time, can yield superstar careers.

And finally, when it comes to dealing with your top performers, do what you can to let them run free. I've seen lots of managers get overly involved with their best salespeople, in effect 'fixing what isn't broken.' You should do what you can, of course, to encourage their continued success and use their triumphs to teach others. But beyond that, I've found that it's best to let them do what they do, without worrying too much about how many calls or visits they're making. Your most valuable people are self-motivated; they won't need you to point the way forward.

Simple as they are, goal setting and time management are the backbones of top achievers. Take the lessons in this book, foster them in your staff, and then enjoy the results!

Carl Henry is a sales educator, keynote speaker and corporate consultant. During the course of his own successful career, he developed The MODERN Sales System, which he has been sharing with companies and associations around the world for many years.

A Certified Speaking Professional and a member of the National Speakers Association, Carl teaches essential sales skills with humor, insight and personal experience. Hundreds of companies throughout a diverse range of industries have used his highly-acclaimed seminars to educate and inspire their sales teams.

Carl's other books include The MODERN Sales System, 15 Hot Tips That Will Supercharge Your Sales Career, The PEOPLE Approach to Customer Service, Sell Something Everyday, 52 Things Every Sales Manager Needs to Know, and High Energy Sales Thoughts.

He currently lives in Charlotte, North Carolina.

To order additional copies of this book, or find out about Carl's seminars contact him at:

Henry Associates
704-847-7390
9430 Valley Road Charlotte, NC 28270
chenry@carlhenry.com
www.carlhenry.com

To order additional copies of this book contact:

Henry Associates
704-847-7390
9430 Valley Road Charlotte, NC 28270
chenry@carlhenry.com
www.carlhenry.com

Printed in the United States
151317LV00001B/5/P